The original hails from Italy, but the modern pizza takes on a variety of delicious forms worldwide. Be it a nice slice or a deep-dish pie, the only thing that hasn't changed since its invention is pizza's everlasting appeal...

now you're cookin'
PIZZA

THIS BOOK JUST MAKES YOU WANNA COOK -

REBO
PUBLISHERS

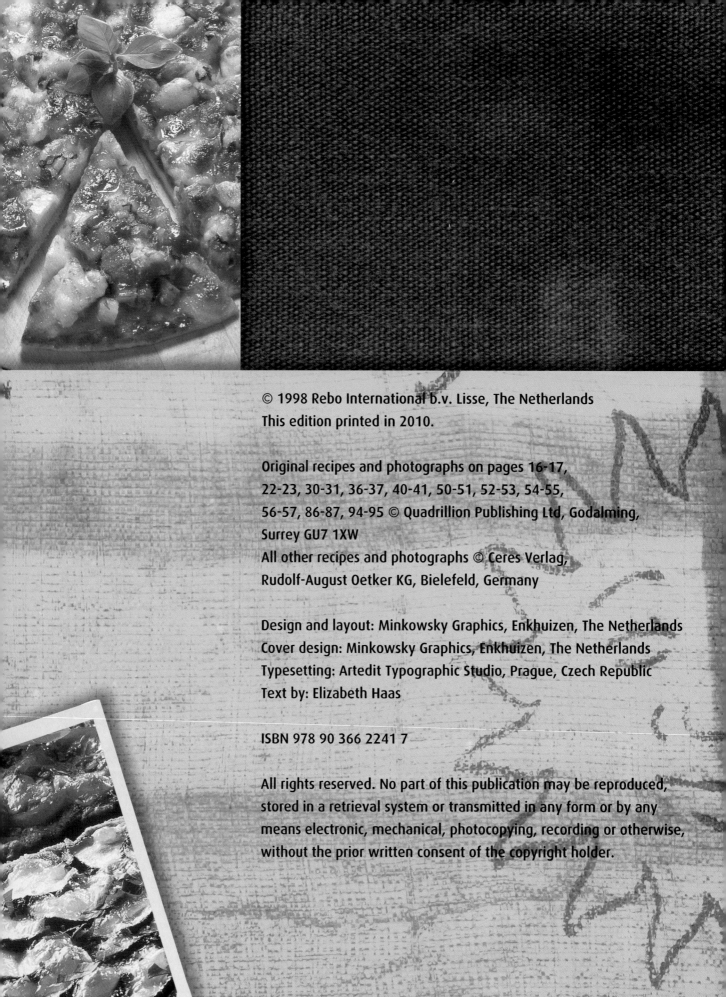

© 1998 Rebo International b.v. Lisse, The Netherlands
This edition printed in 2010.

Original recipes and photographs on pages 16-17,
22-23, 30-31, 36-37, 40-41, 50-51, 52-53, 54-55,
56-57, 86-87, 94-95 © Quadrillion Publishing Ltd, Godalming,
Surrey GU7 1XW
All other recipes and photographs © Ceres Verlag,
Rudolf-August Oetker KG, Bielefeld, Germany

Design and layout: Minkowsky Graphics, Enkhuizen, The Netherlands
Cover design: Minkowsky Graphics, Enkhuizen, The Netherlands
Typesetting: Artedit Typographic Studio, Prague, Czech Republic
Text by: Elizabeth Haas

ISBN 978 90 366 2241 7

now you're cookin'

PIZZA

Foreword

Pizza was born in Naples, Italy, but its fame has now spread far and wide throughout the world. So much so that many countries have all but claimed it as their own, with the U.S. alone boasting the New York "slice" and the Chicago "deep dish". The original simplicity of pizza in its most basic form, thin bread dough topped with cheese, onions, olives, anchovies, or mushrooms, has certainly been surpassed by elaborate combinations of ingredients, some gourmet (caviar and lobster) and some just plain bizzare (pickles and pasta). Pizza crust, however, was originally meant as the perfect base for a harmonious composition of fresh, flavorful ingredients.

For the best results, start with a homemade crust. It isn't complicated to do and is well worth the effort. If you are short on time you'll find plenty of mixes or ready-prepared crusts at the supermarket. Always make sure that you heat the oven to the correct temperature. Pizzas need a very hot oven to ensure a light, crisp finish.

Whether it's a quick-and-easy pizza topped with ingredients you've got on hand (Ham, Pepper, and Mushroom Mini Pizzas), or a more luxurious dish for a special occasion (Seafood Pizza), this book offers a wide range of exciting recipes to choose from. In addition, we've included innovative recipes for stuffed breads with delicious fillings, as well as recipes for quiches and savory flans baked in the oven to golden-brown perfection. And of course, the classics are here, too. For a taste of pizza, old style, you can't go wrong with the Pizza di Napoli.

U.S. KITCHEN CONVERSION
(LIQUID OR VOLUME, APPROXIMATE)

1 tsp. = 1/3 tbsp./5 ml
1 tbsp. = 1/2 fl. oz./15 ml
2 tbsp. = 1 fl. oz./30 ml
1/4 cup = 2 fl. oz./60 ml
1/3 cup = 2 2/3 fl. oz./79 ml
1/2 cup = 4 fl. oz./118 ml
2/3 cup = 5 1/3 fl. oz./158 ml
3/4 cup = 6 fl. oz./177 ml
7/8 cup = 7 fl. oz./207 ml
1 cup = 8 fl. oz./237 ml

Exotic Pizza

Serves 4-6 people

INGREDIENTS
FOR THE DOUGH
2 cups (255 g) plain flour
1 egg
1/2 tsp. salt
6 pats (100 g) cold butter
5 tbsp. buttermilk

FOR THE TOPPING
3 1/2 oz. (99 g) pork filet
1/2 tsp. sugar
freshly ground black pepper
2 tbsp. soy sauce

5 canned pineapple rings
4 small tomatoes
1 head of chicory
2 tbsp. spring onion rings
9 oz. (255 g) Edam cheese

VARIATIONS
Use canned apricot or peach slices in place
of pineapple.

PREPARATION

For the dough, mix the flour, egg, salt, butter, and buttermilk together in a bowl using your fingers or the dough hook on a mixer until a smooth dough has formed. Form the dough into a ball, cover with cling film, and place in the refrigerator for 30 minutes. Grease a baking sheet, then roll out the dough into a large circle. Set aside.

Meanwhile, for the topping, cut the pork into thin slices. In a bowl, stir the sugar and pepper into the soy sauce, add the pork, and stir to mix. Set aside to marinate for 20 minutes.

Drain the pineapple rings. Cut the tomatoes into 8 segments, removing the cores. Dice the chicory.

Cover the pizza base with the slices of pork, spring onion, pineapple, tomatoes, and chicory. Cut the cheese into thin slices and arrange over the top. Bake in a preheated oven at 400°F (200°C) for about 30 minutes, until cooked and golden brown. Serve hot or cold.

Pizza
with Chicken

Serves 4–6 people

8

PREPARATION

Wash and trim the celery and leek, then cut into thick slices.
Seed and slice the red bell pepper, then cut into thin strips.
Peel and thinly slice the onion.

Heat the sunflower oil in a pan, add the celery, leek, pepper, and onion
and cook gently for about 5 minutes, stirring occasionally.
Season the vegetables with salt and pepper and the dried herbs to taste.
Remove the pan from the heat and set aside to cool.

Rinse and dry the chicken pieces and thinly slice. Season with salt
and pepper and dried herbs to taste. Heat the olive oil in a pan,
add the chicken and fry for 3–5 minutes, stirring frequently.
Add tomato ketchup to taste and set aside to cool.

Make up the pizza dough according to the instructions on the packet.
Roll out to a square measuring about 12 x 12 inches (30 x 30 cm) and
place on a greased baking sheet. Sprinkle the contents of the bouquet
garni sachet over the pizza base and spread the vegetables and chicken
on top. Grate the cheese and sprinkle over the pizza. Season with dried
herbs to taste. Drizzle a little olive oil over the pizza and bake
in a preheated oven at 400–425°F (200–220°C) for 25 minutes,
until golden and bubbling. Serve hot.

INGREDIENTS

1 1/2 cups (220 g) celery, sliced
1 leek, sliced
1 red bell pepper
1 onion
3 tbsp. sunflower oil
salt and freshly ground black pepper
dried herbes de Provence, to taste
12 oz. (375 g) skinless, boneless chicken pieces
2 tbsp. olive oil, plus extra for drizzling
tomato ketchup, to taste

1 packet pizza dough mix
1 bouquet garni sachet
5 1/2 oz. (150 g) Gouda cheese

Salami and Artichoke Pizza

Serves 4-6 people

PREPARATION

Preheat oven to 450°F (220°C). For the filling empty, the can of tomatoes into a heated pan. Allow to simmer for 10–15 minutes without a lid so that the tomatoes thicken. Set the pan aside while preparing crust.

Mix the flour, salt, yeast, and sugar in a large bowl.
Make a hole in the middle. Mix the oil with ¾ cup (6 fl. oz. /170 ml) lukewarm water. Pour the mixture slowly into the hole while stirring from the edges in order to make a dough. Add more water if needed. Place the dough on a light surface and knead it for 10 minutes or until smooth and elastic. Roll the dough into a round disc with a diameter of 12 inches (30 cm). Place on a greased baking tray and lift the edge slightly, using your fingers.

Spread the cooked tomato over the pizza base and place the salami or pepperoni, artichoke, plum tomatoes, mozzarella, and olives on top. Bake the pizza 20–25 minutes in the preheated oven until the crust is golden brown.

INGREDIENTS

FOR THE CRUST

1 1/2 cups (350 g) flour
1 tsp. salt
1 packet dried yeast
pinch fine granulated sugar
2 tbsp. olive oil, extra virgin,
plus a little extra for greasing pan
3/4 cup (6 fl. oz./177 ml) lukewarm water

FOR THE FILLING

14 oz. (400 g) can of tomatoes with herbs,
finely chopped
3 1/2 oz. (85 g) pepper salami
or pepperoni, cut into strips
10 oz. (285 g) can
of artichokes, drained
9 oz. (250 g) plum tomatoes,
cut lengthwise
3 1/2 oz. (100 g) mozzarella,
cut into cubes
2 oz. (40 g) black olives, pitted

Bacon, Potato, and Tomato Pizza

Serves 4 people

PREPARATION

Peel and wash the potatoes and cut into thin, round slices.
Dry on absorbent kitchen paper and set aside. Dice the bacon and fry
in a pan until sealed all over. Add the slices of potato once the bacon
has released its fat and cook for about 5 minutes, stirring occasionally.

Slice the tomatoes, then mix with the potatoes and arrange evenly
on a greased baking sheet. Sprinkle with oregano, parsley, garlic salt,
and black pepper to taste. Lay slices of cheese evenly on top
of the mixture. Bake in a preheated oven at 400°F (200°C)
for 25 minutes. Serve immediately, garnished with fresh herb sprigs.

INGREDIENTS

1 lb. 10 oz. (750 g) potatoes
4 slices bacon
3 large tomatoes
1/4 tsp. dried oregano
1 tbsp. finely chopped fresh parsley
garlic salt
freshly ground black pepper
9 oz. (250 g) Emmenthal cheese, sliced
fresh herb sprigs, to garnish

SERVING SUGGESTION

Serve with thick slices of fresh
crusty French bread.

VARIATIONS

Use sweet potatoes in place of
standard potatoes. Use smoked
bacon for extra flavor. Use basil
or tarragon in place of parsley.

Pizza di Napoli

Serves 6-8 people

INGREDIENTS
FOR THE DOUGH

1/2 cup (99 g) low-fat cottage cheese
4 tbsp. milk
4 tbsp. olive oil, 1 1/2 tsp. salt
1 1/2 cups (198 g) plain flour
1 tbsp. baking powder

FOR THE TOPPING

4 tbsp. olive oil
1/2 cup (4 fl. oz/118 ml) tomato
ketchup
2x 14-oz. (800 g) cans chopped

tomatoes,
drained, 1 lb. 9 oz. (700 g) canned,
sliced mushrooms, drained
2 onions, sliced, 1 tsp. salt
1 tsp. freshly ground black pepper
1 tsp. dried oregano, 12 slices salami
3 1/2 oz. (100 g) mozzarella cheese,
thinly sliced

PREPARATION

For the dough, mix the cottage cheese, milk, oil, and salt together in a bowl. Sift the flour and baking powder on top and fold into the cottage cheese mixture. Once the dough has been formed, shape into a ball and place on a greased baking sheet. Roll out the dough until it fills the whole baking sheet.

For the topping, mix the oil with the tomato ketchup and spread over the dough. Cover the pizza base with the tomatoes, mushrooms, and onions and season with salt and pepper. Sprinkle oregano over the vegetables, then arrange slices of salami over the pizza and cover with the cheese slices.

Bake in a preheated oven at 400°F (200°C) for about 30 minutes, until golden brown and bubbling. Serve hot.

Ham, Pepper, and Mushroom Mini Pizzas

Makes 20 mini pizzas

PREPARATION

For the dough, place the flour in a mixing bowl and make a well in the center. Add the yeast and mix with the flour. Pour ½ cup (4 fl. oz./118 ml) lukewarm water into the well, mix well, then cover and set aside for 20 minutes. Mix in the butter, salt, and egg using a dough hook on a mixer or your hands and knead the dough until it has a smooth consistency. Put in a warm place and set aside until risen and doubled in size. Knead the dough again, then set aside.

For the topping, peel the onions and thinly slice. Heat the oil in a pan, add the onion and cook until softened. Add the tomatoes, cover the pan and leave to simmer for 15–20 minutes, stirring occasionally. Cut the peppers in half and remove and discard the stems, seeds, and cores, then thinly slice. Clean the mushrooms and cut into thin slices. Add the peppers and mushrooms to the tomatoes and cook for a further 5 minutes, stirring once or twice.

Slice the ham into thin strips and add to the tomatoes. Add salt and pepper, oregano and basil to taste. Divide the dough into 20 equal pieces, roll out each piece as thinly as possible and place on a greased baking sheet. Cover each mini pizza with the tomato topping and sprinkle with grated cheese. Bake in a preheated oven at 400°F (200°C) for about 25 minutes, until risen and golden brown. Serve hot.

INGREDIENTS

FOR THE DOUGH

4 cups (500 g) strong plain white flour
3 tsp. fresh yeast, 3 tbsp. butter
1/4 tsp. salt, 1 egg

FOR THE TOPPING

2 onions, 1 tbsp. olive oil
2 x 14 oz. (800 g) cans chopped tomatoes
1 red bell pepper, 1 green bell pepper
7 oz. (220 g) mushrooms

3 oz. (100 g) lean cooked ham
salt and freshly ground black pepper
chopped fresh marjoram or oregano, to taste
chopped fresh basil, to taste
7 oz. (200 g) mature Cheddar cheese, grated

Ham and Mozzarella Pizza

Serves 4 people

INGREDIENTS

salt and freshly ground black pepper
1 quantity bread dough (page 57)
2 tomatoes, sliced, 1/2 onion,
thinly sliced
2 slices lean cooked ham,
cut into small pieces
7 oz. (200 g) mozzarella cheese
salt and freshly ground black pepper
1 tsp. dried oregano

FOR THE TOMATO SAUCE
2 tbsp. olive oil
1 onion, finely chopped
4 large tomatoes, seeded,
skinned, and finely chopped
1 bay leaf, 1 small sprig of thyme
dash Tabasco sauce
1 clove garlic, finely chopped

PREPARATION

To make the tomato sauce, heat the oil in a frying pan and fry the onion until softened. Add the tomatoes, bay leaf, thyme, Tabasco, and garlic. Season with salt and pepper and cook for about 30 minutes, stirring frequently.

When the liquid from the tomatoes has almost evaporated, remove and discard the bay leaf and the sprig of thyme. Allow the sauce to cool a little, then blend in a food processor until smooth. Roll out the dough into a round, place on a baking sheet and spread with the prepared tomato sauce.

Lay the sliced tomatoes over the tomato sauce, then top with the onion and ham. Cut the cheese into thin slices and lay the slices over the pizza. Season with salt and pepper and sprinkle over the oregano. Cook in a preheated oven at 425°F (225°C) for about 15 minutes. Serve immediately.

Neapolitan Pizza

Serves 4 people

PREPARATION

Sift the flour into a mixing bowl and add the yeast, sugar, salt, ½ cup (4. fl. oz./118 ml) warm water, and olive oil. Knead the mixture for about 5 minutes to form a smooth dough. Cover the bowl with a damp warm cloth and set aside in a warm place for 30 minutes, until risen. Knead the dough thoroughly on a lightly floured work surface before rolling out thinly into a large rectangle. Place on a greased baking sheet and prick with a fork.

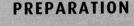

Spread the pizza base with tomato purée and place the sliced tomatoes on top. Cut the ham and salami into thin strips and place over the tomatoes. Scatter the olives over the meat, top with anchovy filets, then season with pepper, oregano or marjoram and basil to taste. Arrange the cheese on top. Bake in a preheated oven at 425°F (220°C) for 20–25 minutes, until cooked and golden brown. Serve hot, garnished with chopped fresh parsley.

INGREDIENTS

1 1/4 cups (200 g) strong plain white flour
1/2 tbsp. yeast
1 tsp. sugar
salt

1 tbsp. olive oil, 1 tbsp. tomato purée
1 large tomato, sliced, 1 oz. (25 g) boiled ham
1 oz. salami
6–8 black and green olives
6–8 anchovy filets
freshly ground black pepper

finely chopped fresh oregano
or marjoram, to taste
finely chopped fresh basil,
to taste
3 oz. (85 g) mozzarella cheese,
sliced
2 tbsp. finely chopped fresh
parsley

Bacon and Goat Cheese Pizza

Serves 4 people

INGREDIENTS

1 quantity bread dough (page 57)
1 quantity tomato sauce (page 18)
1 onion, thinly sliced
4 slices bacon
goat cheese
salt and freshly ground black
pepper
1 tbsp. fresh marjoram, chopped
black olives, to garnish

PREPARATION

Roll out the dough thinly on a lightly floured work surface. Place on a greased baking sheet. Spread the tomato sauce over the dough, then sprinkle over the onion. Cut the bacon into small pieces and scatter over the pizza. Thinly slice the goat cheese and lay the slices over the bacon.

Season with salt and pepper, sprinkle over the marjoram and bake in a preheated oven at 425°F (220°C) for about 15 minutes. Serve hot, garnished with olives.

SERVING SUGGESTION

Serve with a mixed leaf salad tossed in chili or herb oil.

VARIATIONS

Use smoked bacon for extra flavor.
Use flaked tuna or salmon
in place of bacon.

COOK'S TIP

Use a finely serrated knife when cutting the goat cheese. This helps prevent it from crumbling.

Individual Egg and Bacon Pizzas

Serves 4 people

24

PREPARATION

Form the dough into 4 equal balls. Roll out each ball on a lightly floured work surface into a thin round. Spread about 5 tablespoons of the tomato sauce over each pizza base.

Sprinkle the onion over the tomato sauce, then the bacon. Season with salt and pepper. Break one egg onto the center of each pizza. Sprinkle the cheese evenly over the pizza topping on each pizza.
Bake in a preheated oven at 425°F (220°C) for about 10–15 minutes.
Serve immediately.

COOK'S TIPS

If you prefer your egg yolks to remain runny, break the eggs onto the pizzas halfway through the cooking time. Do not spread the egg white out onto the pizza – the egg will spread over the pizza by itself during cooking.

INGREDIENTS

1 quantity bread dough (page 57)
1 quantity tomato sauce (page 18)
1 large onion, finely sliced
4 slices bacon, cut into small pieces
salt and freshly ground black pepper
4 eggs
4 tbsp. grated Parmesan cheese

SERVING SUGGESTION

Serve with a tossed mixed salad.

VARIATIONS

Use prosciutto or Parma ham
in place of bacon.
Use Gruyère cheese in place
of Parmesan.

Spinach, Ham, and Bacon Pizza

Serves 4–6 people

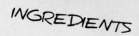

INGREDIENTS

7/8 cup (175 g) strong plain white flour

7/8 cup (175 g) coarsely ground wheat

1 tsp. yeast, 2 tbsp. butter

1/2 tsp. sugar

salt and freshly ground black pepper

1/2 cup (4 fl. oz./118 ml) lukewarm milk

1 onion, 2 slices bacon

2 slices ham, 2 tbsp. olive oil

1 lb. 2 oz. (500 g) fresh spinach

ground nutmeg, to taste

lemon juice, to taste

3 large tomatoes

chopped fresh marjoram, to taste

5 1/2 oz. (150 g) Gouda cheese

PREPARATION

Sift the flour into a mixing bowl, add the ground wheat, yeast, butter, sugar, salt and pepper, and milk. Knead to a smooth dough. Cover and set aside the dough in a warm place until risen and doubled in size. Knead the dough again, then roll out into a round about 14 inches (35 cm) in diameter and place on a greased baking sheet.

Peel the onion, then slice and finely chop. Chop the bacon and ham into small cubes. Heat the oil in a pan and cook the onion, bacon and ham for 5 minutes, stirring occasionally. Wash the spinach and add to the pan with nutmeg and lemon juice to taste. Cook for 3 minutes. Squeeze out the excess fluid from the spinach, then spread over the pizza base.

Slice the tomatoes, lay on top of the spinach and season with salt and pepper and marjoram to taste. Grate the cheese and sprinkle over the pizza. Bake in a preheated oven 425°F (220°C) for 25–30 minutes. Serve hot.

Pizza
with Monkfish

Serves 4–6 people

PREPARATION

Sift the flour into a bowl and add a large pinch of salt. Make a well in the center of the flour and crumble in the yeast. Add about ½ cup (4 fl. oz./118 ml) lukewarm water and the sunflower oil and stir to dissolve the yeast. Set aside for 10 minutes before kneading the mixture to a smooth dough. Cover the bowl and set aside in a warm place for about 1 hour, until risen and doubled in size.

Cut the fish into cubes and set aside. Heat the olive oil in a pan and cook the shallots and celery until softened. Add the fish and tomatoes and season to taste with salt and pepper. Add the garlic and basil and stir to mix. Cook gently for 5 minutes, stirring occasionally.

Roll out the dough on a lightly floured work surface into a large circle and place on a greased baking sheet. Drizzle the pizza base with a little olive and spread the fish mixture on top. Bake in a preheated oven at 425°F (220°C) for about 20 minutes, until risen and cooked. Serve hot, garnished with fresh basil sprigs.

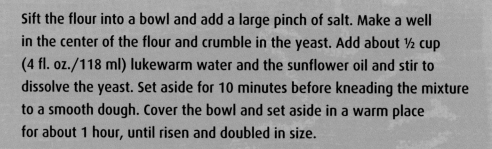

INGREDIENTS

2 cups (255 g) strong white plain flour
salt and freshly ground black pepper
1 tbsp. fresh yeast
1/2 tsp. sunflower oil
14 oz. (400 g) skinless, boneless monkfish
4 tbsp. olive oil, plus extra for drizzling
4 shallots, finely chopped
1 1/2 cup (200 g) celery, cut into strips
1 large tomato, cut into chunks

1 clove garlic, thinly sliced
5 fresh basil leaves
fresh basil sprigs, to garnish

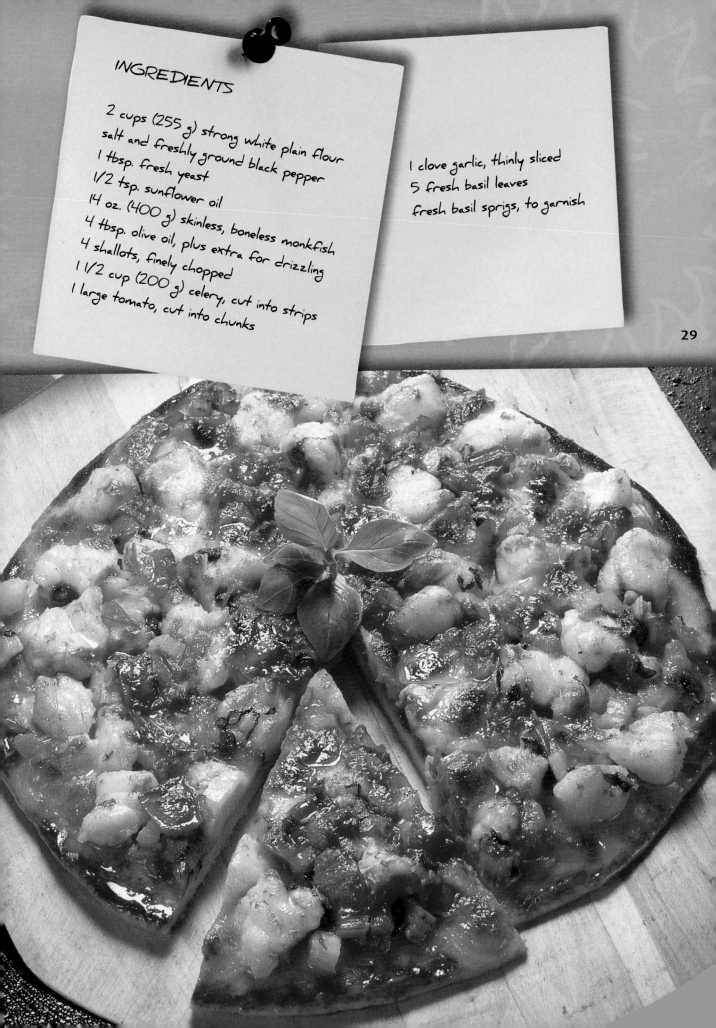

Anchovy and Onion Pizza

Serves 4 people

PREPARATION

Roll out the dough into 2 rounds. Place on 2 greased baking sheets. Spread the tomato sauce evenly over the 2 pizzas. Place the sliced onion over the sauce and lay the anchovy filets neatly over the onion.

Season with salt and pepper. Sprinkle over the dried onion and cook in a preheated oven at 425°F (200°C) for about 20 minutes, or until crisp and cooked. Serve immediately, garnished with fresh herb sprigs.

SERVING SUGGESTION

As you serve the pizzas, sprinkle over a little hot peppered olive oil. Alternatively, add a drop or two of Tabasco to the tomato sauce.

VARIATIONS

Use 2 large leeks in place of onions. Use dried or chopped fresh garlic in place of dried onion.

INGREDIENTS

1 quantity bread dough (page 57)
1 quantity tomato sauce (page 18)
2 large onions, thinly sliced
16 anchovy filets
salt and freshly ground black pepper
1 tsp. dried onion
fresh herb sprigs, to garnish

COOK'S TIP

To allow for the elasticity of the dough, roll the rounds larger than desired and leave them for a minute to settle before spreading with the tomato sauce.

Mini Shrimp Pizzas

Serves 6 people

PREPARATION

In a bowl, carefully mix the yeast with the flour, then add
the salt, sugar, olive oil, and ½ cup (4 fl. oz./118 ml) lukewarm
water. Mix thoroughly to form a smooth dough.
Knead the dough for about 5 minutes, then cover and set aside
in a warm place until risen and doubled in size. Divide the dough
into 6 equal portions and roll out each one into a round.
Place on greased baking sheets.

Spread the shrimp evenly over the pizza bases and set aside.
In a bowl, beat the egg into the sour cream, stir in the
seasonings and cover the shrimp evenly with the sauce.
Sprinkle the pizzas with chopped parsley and grated Parmesan.
Bake in a preheated oven at 425°F (220°C) for 20 minutes,
until risen and cooked. Serve hot.

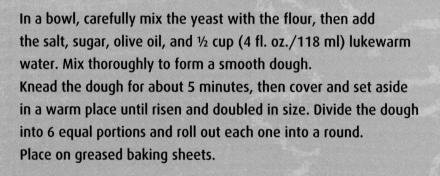

INGREDIENTS

pinch fresh yeast
1 cup plus 1 tbsp. (255 g) strong plain white flour
1/2 tsp. salt
1/2 tsp. sugar
2 tbsp. olive oil
10 1/2 oz. (300 g) cooked, shelled shrimp
1 egg
1 tbsp. sour cream
salt and freshly ground white pepper
lemon pepper

3 tbsp. fresh parsley
1/2 cup plus 1 tbsp. (50 g) fresh Parmesan cheese, grated

VARIATIONS

Use half white and half wholemeal flour in place of all white flour. Use chopped fresh basil or cilantro in place of parsley. Use cooked, shelled mussels in place of shrimp.

Pizza Marinara

PREPARATION

Mix the tomato purée with the wine, 1 tablespoon water, spring onions, oregano, garlic, and salt and pepper. Spread over halved muffins mixture.

Arrange the shellfish on top with a cross of anchovies. Add the olives and capers and sprinkle with the mozzarella cheese. Sprinkle the Parmesan cheese on last and arrange the pizzas on a grill rack in a grill pan.

Place under a preheated grill for a few minutes, until the cheese is melted and bubbling. Serve hot.

INGREDIENTS

4 tbsp. tomato purée
1 tbsp. dry white wine
2 spring onions, chopped
1/2 tsp. dried oregano
1 clove garlic, crushed
salt and freshly ground black pepper
4 English muffins, split in half
4 oz. (15 g) cooked, shelled shrimp,
canned or frozen mussels, canned or fresh
clams or cockles or a combination of all 3
8 anchovy filets
4 black olives, pitted and sliced
2 tsp. capers
1/3 cup (85 g) mozzarella cheese, grated
2 tbsp. Parmesan cheese, grated

COOK'S TIP

You can pre-cook the pizzas and freeze them for later use. Use fresh seafood and canned tuna. Let the pizzas thaw completely before grilling.

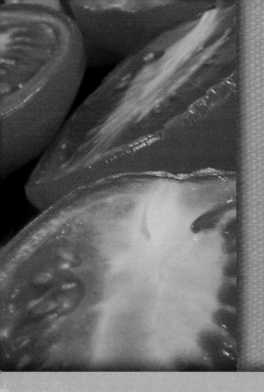

Pizza
San Domenico

PREPARATION

For the dough, sift the flour into a bowl and mix in the dried yeast.
Add the olive oil, salt, sugar, and ½ cup (4 fl. oz./118 ml) lukewarm
water. Mix to a dough, then knead for about 5 minutes, until smooth.
Cover the dough and set aside in a warm place until risen and doubled
in size.

Knead the dough again, then divide into 4 equal pieces. Roll out each
piece to form an 8-inch (20 cm) round pizza base. Place on a greased
baking sheet. Fold up the edge of each pizza base to form a raised rim
and brush the dough with olive oil.

For the topping, slice the tomatoes and drizzle with olive oil, then
arrange the slices over the pizza bases. Top with the garlic, then
the slices of mozzarella cheese and season with pepper. Make a cross
of anchovy filets on each pizza, then leave the pizzas in a warm place
to rise again. Sprinkle with Parmesan cheese, then bake in a preheated
oven at 375°F (190°C) for 15 minutes, until risen and golden brown.
Serve hot, garnished with fresh marjoram sprigs.

INGREDIENTS

FOR THE DOUGH

3 cups (370 g) strong plain white flour
1 sachet dried yeast
4 tbsp. olive oil, plus extra for brushing
1 tsp. salt, 1 tsp. sugar

FOR THE TOPPING

1 large tomato, skinned
3 tbsp. olive oil
6 peeled cloves garlic, thinly sliced

7 oz. (200 g) mozzarella cheese, sliced
freshly ground black pepper
10 anchovy filets
1/4 cup (150 g) grated Parmesan cheese
fresh marjoram sprigs, to garnish

Pizza with Mussels

Serves 2–4 people

INGREDIENTS

FOR THE DOUGH

2 3/4 cups (300 g) strong plain white flour
1 sachet dried yeast
4 tbsp. olive oil, 1 tsp. salt
1/2 cup (4 fl. oz./118 ml) lukewarm milk

FOR THE TOPPING

9 oz. (255 g) cooked mushrooms

4 slices lean cooked ham
1 lb. 2 oz. (500 g) cooked, shelled mussels
4 tomatoes, skinned
9 oz. (250 g) mozzarella cheese
10 stuffed Spanish olives
5 small fresh chilis
1/2 tbsp. green peppercorns
1/2 tsp. oregano
1/2 tsp. each of basil, sage, and rosemary
4 tbsp. olive oil

PREPARATION

For the dough, sift the flour into a bowl and mix in the dried yeast thoroughly before adding the olive oil, salt, and lukewarm milk, to form a dough. Knead the dough for about 5 minutes. If the dough is too sticky, sprinkle over a little extra flour but take care not to add too much so that the dough remains workable. Set aside the dough in a warm place until risen and doubled in size. Knead the dough again and divide in half. Roll out each half of dough to make 2 pizza bases about 8 inches (20 cm) in diameter. Place on a greased baking sheet.

For the topping, slice the cooked mushrooms in half, chop the ham, mussels, tomatoes, and cheese and slice the stuffed olives. Slice the chilis into rings. Distribute all the topping ingredients evenly over the 2 pizza bases.

Sprinkle the green peppercorns, oregano, basil, sage, and rosemary over the topping, then drizzle over the olive oil. Bake in a preheated oven at 425°F (220°C) for about 25 minutes, until golden and bubbling. Serve hot.

Seafood Pizza

Serves 4 people

PREPARATION

Wash, brush, and rinse the cockles and mussels thoroughly.
Place them in a large saucepan, pour over the wine and place
on high heat, shaking the pan frequently until all the shells have
opened. Set the pan aside to allow the contents to cool.
Once the cockles and mussels are cooled, remove from their
shells, discarding any that have not opened. Discard the juices.

Roll out the bread dough into a large round on a lightly floured
work surface. Place on a baking sheet. Pour the tomato sauce
into the center of the pizza and spread over the dough
with the back of a spoon.

Place the sliced onion over the tomato sauce, then place
the mussels and cockles on top. Scatter over the garlic, season
with marjoram and salt and pepper and top with Parmesan cheese.

Cook in a preheated oven at 425°F (220°C) for about
15–25 minutes, depending on the thickness of the dough.
Serve immediately.

INGREDIENTS

8 oz. (225 g) fresh cockles
1 lb. (450 g) fresh mussels
½ cup (4 fl. oz/118 ml) white wine
1 quantity bread dough (page 57)
1 quantity tomato sauce (page 18)
1 large onion, thinly sliced
2 cloves garlic, chopped
1 tsp. dried marjoram

salt and freshly ground
black pepper
4 tbsp. grated Parmesan
cheese

Tomato, Zucchini, and Carrot Pizzas

Makes 12 pizzas

PREPARATION

Dissolve the yeast in 2–3 tablespoon lukewarm water. Make a dough by mixing the flour in a bowl with the yeast mixture, 1 cup (8 fl. oz./237 ml) lukewarm water, corn oil, and ½ teaspoon salt. Wash, dry, and finely chop the parsley and wild sorrel. Peel the garlic, thinly slice, then knead into the dough with the herbs. Cover the dough and set aside in a warm place. When the dough has risen, divide into 12 equal portions and roll or form into 12 small thin pizza bases. Place on 2 baking sheets.

Cut the carrots into ¼-inch (1 ¼ cm) slices. Heat 1 tablespoon sunflower oil, add salt, and cook the carrots gently for about 10 minutes, until tender, stirring occasionally. Slice the tomatoes and zucchinis into ¼-inch (1 ¼ cm) slices. Dice the cheese into small cubes. Cover 4 pizzas with zucchinis, 4 with carrots, and 4 with tomatoes, then top each pizza with cheese and season with salt and pepper.

Bake in preheated oven at 400°F (200°C) for 25–30 minutes. When cooked, sprinkle with the remaining sunflower oil and garnish with chopped basil. Serve hot, garnished with fresh basil sprigs.

INGREDIENTS

1 1/2 tbsp. fresh yeast
2 3/4 cup (300 g) strong wholemeal
flour, 1 tbsp. corn oil, salt
1 bunch of fresh parsley
1 bunch of wild sorrel
2 cloves garlic, 5 medium carrots
5 tbsp. sunflower oil
2 large tomatoes
2 small zucchinis
10 1/2 oz. (300 g) mozzarella cheese
freshly ground black pepper

1 tbsp. finely chopped fresh basil
fresh basil sprigs, to garnish

SERVING SUGGESTION

Serve with a pepper and onion salad
and fresh crusty bread.

VARIATIONS

Use leeks in place of carrots. Use fresh
chives in place of parsley. Use baby
eggplant in place of zucchinis.

43

Mushroom Pizza

Serves 4 people

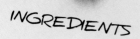

INGREDIENTS

2 cups (255 g) strong plain white flour

1 1/2 tbsp. fresh yeast

1/2 tsp. sunflower oil

1 onion

1 clove garlic

2 tbsp. olive oil, plus extra for drizzling

2x 14-oz. (800 g) cans tomatoes

1 tbsp. chopped fresh basil

salt and freshly ground black pepper

2 cups (10 1/2 oz./300 g) mushrooms

10 1/2 oz. (300 g) mozzarella cheese, sliced

chopped fresh parsley, for sprinkling

PREPARATION

Sift the flour into a bowl and make a well in the center. Crumble in the yeast and add ½ cup (4 fl. oz./118 ml) lukewarm water and sunflower oil to dissolve the yeast. Work into a dough, then cover and leave in a warm place for about 1 hour, until risen and doubled in size.

Peel the onion and garlic and thinly slice. Heat the olive oil in a pan and fry the onion and garlic until softened. Add the tomatoes and their juice and mash with a fork. Sprinkle in the basil and salt and pepper and allow to heat through, stirring occasionally.

Roll out the dough on a lightly floured work surface and place on a greased baking sheet. Spread the tomato sauce over the pizza base. Slice the mushrooms and arrange over the pizza base. Top with the cheese. Drizzle a little olive oil over the topping and sprinkle with chopped parsley. Bake in a preheated oven at 425°F (220°C) for about 20 minutes, until cooked and golden brown. Serve hot.

Onion and Cheese Pizza

Serves 4 people

PREPARATION

For the dough, sift the flour into a mixing bowl and mix
in the dried yeast, ground coriander, salt, ground caraway seeds,
eggs, milk, and butter. Knead to form a smooth dough,
then coverand set aside in a warm place until risen and doubled
in size. Knead the dough again, then roll out onto a greased
baking sheet. Set aside.

For the topping, peel the onions and finely chop. Melt the butter
in a pan, add the onions, and cook until softened.
Set aside to cool.

Slice the tomatoes and set aside. Trim the chilis, remove
the seeds and slice into rings. Coarsely grate the cheese.
Arrange all the topping ingredients over the pizza base.
For the sauce, place the sour cream, whipping cream, eggs, flour,
salt, and pepper, and nutmeg to taste in a mixer and blend.

Pour the mixture over the pizza topping, then sprinkle
with caraway seeds. Place the baking sheet in a cold oven,
then bake at 400°F (200°C) for about 50 minutes. Serve hot.

INGREDIENTS

FOR THE DOUGH

4 cups (500 g) strong wholemeal flour
1 sachet dried yeast, 1 tsp. ground coriander
1 tsp. sea salt, 1 tsp. ground caraway seeds
2 eggs, 3/4 cup (6 fl. oz./175 ml) lukewarm
milk, 5 tbsp. butter, melted then cooled

FOR THE TOPPING

1 3/4 cup (200g) onions, 2 tbsp. butter,
2 large beefsteak tomatoes, 4 fresh chilis

3 1/2 cups (400 g)
Emmenthal cheese

FOR THE SAUCE

1 cup (237 g) sour cream
1 cup (8 fl. oz./237 ml) heavy cream
3 eggs, 3 tbsp. wholemeal flour
1 tsp. sea salt, freshly ground black
pepper, to taste, ground nutmeg, to
taste, 2–3 tbsp. caraway seeds

Artichoke Pizza

PREPARATION

Mix the flour, suet, and salt together in a large bowl and add enough cold water to make a pliable dough. Roll out into a 10-inch (25 cm) round and place on a greased baking sheet. Brush with olive oil and spread with the tomato purée.

Arrange the onion, artichokes, and tomatoes on top. Sprinkle with oregano. Arrange the cheese over the tomatoes and place the olives on top, if using. Bake in a preheated oven at 375°F (190°C) for about 35 minutes. Serve hot.

INGREDIENTS

1 1/2 cups (225 g) wholemeal self-rising flour
3 oz. (85 g) vegetable suet, 1/2 tsp. salt, olive oil
1 tbsp. tomato purée
1 medium onion, very finely chopped
14-oz. (400 g) can artichoke hearts,
drained and halved
6 medium tomatoes, skinned and sliced
1 tsp. dried oregano
4 oz. (115 g) Cheddar cheese, finely sliced
12 black olives, pitted and halved (optional)

Mixed Legume Pizza

Serves 4–8 people

COOK'S TIP

Use canned legumes to save on preparation time.

INGREDIENTS

1 tbsp. fresh yeast, 3 1/3 cup (400 g) strong wholemeal flour, 2 tbsp. walnut oil, 2 onions, 1 tbsp. olive oil, 1 clove garlic salt and freshly ground black pepper 2 lb. 4 oz. (1 kg) tomatoes 1 cup (175 g) cooked red lentils 1 cup (175 g) cooked yellow lentils 1 cup (175 g) cooked peas 1 cup (175 g) cooked chickpeas 2 tbsp. alfalfa shoots 4 tbsp. grated Parmesan cheese

PREPARATION

Dissolve the yeast in 4 tablespoons lukewarm water then add to the flour in a bowl with 1 cup (8 fl. oz./237 ml) lukewarm water and the walnut oil. Knead to a smooth, workable dough and set aside. Peel and chop the onions and cook them in the olive oil in a pan until softened. Peel and crush the garlic and knead into the dough with the onion mixture. Add salt and pepper to taste, form into a ball, cover and set aside in a warm place for about 30 minutes, until risen and doubled in size.

Roll out the dough to form 4 pizza bases, each about 10 inches (25 cm) in diameter. Place on 2 greased baking sheets.

Slice the tomatoes and arrange over the pizza bases. Season with salt and pepper to taste. Spread the mixed lentils over the pizza bases and leave in a warm place to rise for a further 15 minutes.

Bake in a preheated oven at 400°F (200°C) for 20–25 minutes, until cooked and lightly browned. Mix the alfalfa shoots with the cheese and sprinkle over the cooked pizzas just before serving. Serve immediately.

Mixed Vegetable Scone-Based Pizza

Serves 4–6 people

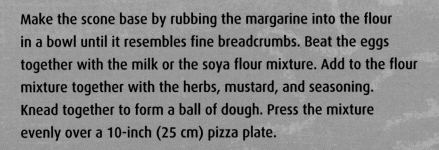

PREPARATION

Make the scone base by rubbing the margarine into the flour
in a bowl until it resembles fine breadcrumbs. Beat the eggs
together with the milk or the soya flour mixture. Add to the flour
mixture together with the herbs, mustard, and seasoning.
Knead together to form a ball of dough. Press the mixture
evenly over a 10-inch (25 cm) pizza plate.

For the topping, brush the top of the pizza base with a little olive
oil and spread the tomato purée evenly over the top
with a knife. Melt the butter in a frying pan and cook
the onions, mushrooms, pepper, and celery for 4–5 minutes,
until softened a little. Pile the mixture on top of the pizza base.
Lay the tomatoes evenly over the top and sprinkle over the
grated cheese. Bake in a preheated oven at 400°F (200°C)
for 20–25 minutes, until the cheese is melted and the pizza
is golden brown. Serve hot, garnished with fresh
watercress sprigs.

INGREDIENTS

FOR THE BASE

1/2 cup (114 g) margarine, 1 2/3 cup (300 g) plain wholemeal flour, 2 small eggs plus 2 tbsp. milk or 4 tbsp. soya flour mixed with 3 tbsp. water, 1/2 tsp. mixed dried herbs, 1/2 tsp. mustard powder salt and freshly ground black pepper

FOR THE TOPPING

A little olive oil, 1 tbsp. tomato purée

4 tbsp. butter
1 large onion, finely chopped
1/2 cup (125 g) mushrooms, sliced
1 green or red bell pepper, thinly sliced
2 sticks celery, thinly sliced
4 tomatoes, sliced
1 cup (155 g) Cheddar cheese, grated
watercress sprigs, to garnish

Mixed Pepper Pizza

Serves 4 people

INGREDIENTS

1 quantity bread dough (page 58)
1 quantity tomato sauce (page 18)
1 red bell pepper, seeded and cut into thin slices, 1 green bell pepper, seeded and cut into thin slices, 1 yellow bell pepper, seeded and cut into thin slices
7 oz. (200 g) mozzarella cheese, sliced
salt and freshly ground black pepper
1 tsp. dried marjoram
a few drops of olive oil

PREPARATION

Roll out the dough into a round on a lightly floured work surface. Place on a greased baking sheet.

Spread the tomato sauce over the dough. Arrange the mixed pepper slices evenly over the tomato sauce. Place slices of cheese over the peppers. Season with salt and pepper and sprinkle over the marjoram. Sprinkle over a little olive oil and bake in a preheated oven at 425°F for (220°C) 10–15 minutes, until golden brown and bubbling. Serve hot.

VARIATIONS

Use mushrooms in place of one of the peppers. Use an onion in place of one of the peppers.

Wild
Mushroom Pizza

PREPARATION

For the dough, mix the yeast, ½ cup (4 fl. oz./118 ml) lukewarm water and milk together in a small bowl. Stir until the yeast dissolves. Place the flour in a large bowl, add the salt, then mix in the yeast mixture. Knead the dough by hand for 3 minutes. Cover with a dish towel and set aside in a warm place for 45 minutes, until risen.

For the topping, heat the butter in a pan and fry the shallot, button mushrooms and garlic for 2 minutes. Roll out the dough on a lightly floured work surface into the desired thickness and shape and place on a greased baking sheet. Spread the tomato sauce evenly over the pizza base, then add the mushroom mixture on top.

Arrange the wild mushrooms over the cooked mushroom mixture, then sprinkle over the Parmesan cheese. Dot the olives over the pizza and season to taste with salt and pepper. Cook in a preheated oven at 425°F (220°C) for 20–30 minutes, until the dough base is crisp and golden brown. Serve immediately.

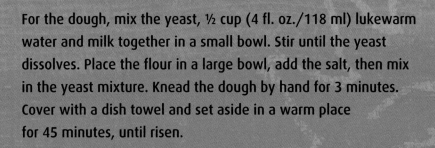

INGREDIENTS

FOR THE BREAD DOUGH

1 tbsp. yeast
1/4 cup (2 fl. oz./60 ml) milk
2 cups (255 g) strong plain
white flour, sifted, pinch of salt

FOR THE TOPPING

4 tbsp. butter, 1 shallot, finely chopped
4 button mushrooms, thinly sliced

1/2 clove garlic, finely chopped
1 1/4 cups (305 g) tomato
sauce (page 18)
1/2 cup (113 g) wild
mushrooms, thinly sliced
2 tbsp. grated Parmesan cheese
20 olives, salt and freshly
ground black pepper

Cossack Rolls

PREPARATION

For the dough, mix the flours and salt together in a bowl.
Dissolve the yeast in 1 ¼ cup (10 fl. oz./300 ml) lukewarm water
and add to the flour with the butter or lard.

Mix well to form a dough, then knead for about 5 minutes, until
a smooth dough is formed. Cover the dough and set aside in a warm
place until risen and doubled in size. For the filling, soak the stale bread
in water, drain well, then place in a bowl with the mince, onion and
herbs. Add the eggs and salt and pepper and paprika to taste. Mix well
and set aside. Knead the dough again on a lightly floured work surface
and divide in half. Roll out each half to about 12 x 14 inches
(30 x 35 cm) and cut into 5 x 6–inch (12 x 15 cm) rectangles.

Spread the herb filling over the pieces of dough, leaving a ¾–inch (2 cm)
border around the edge. Brush the border with water. Roll up each piece
of dough from the longer side and press the seams together.
Place seam-side down on a greased baking sheet. Cover and set aside
in a warm place until the rolls have risen and doubled in size.

Brush the tops of the rolls with a little milk and make zigzag cuts
in the dough. Bake in a preheated oven at 400°F (200°C)
for 30–35 minutes. Serve hot.

INGREDIENTS

FOR THE DOUGH

1 3/4 tbsp. wholemeal rye flour
3 cups (375 g) strong plain white flour
1 tsp salt, 3 tbsp. fresh yeast
3 tbsp. soft butter or lard

FOR THE FILLING

1 slice stale bread
1 lb. 2 oz. (500 g) mixed ground beef
and pork

1 onion, finely chopped
3 tbsp. chopped fresh mixed
herbs
2 eggs
salt and freshly ground
black pepper
paprika, to taste
milk, for brushing

Mushroom-Filled Rolls

PREPARATION

For the dough, mix the flour with the yeast in a bowl, then add the salt, eggs, soft butter, and yogurt and mix well to form a dough. Knead for about 5 minutes until smooth. Cover and set aside in a warm place until risen and doubled in size.

Meanwhile, for the filling, cut the spring onions in 4 lengthways, then thinly slice. Thinly slice the mushrooms. Melt the butter in a pan and cook the spring onions until softened. Add the mushrooms and cook for about 5 minutes. Season to taste with salt and pepper. Cook, uncovered, until all the liquid has evaporated, stirring occasionally.

Remove the pan from the heat and set aside to cool, then mix in the mixed herbs. Adjust the seasoning as required. Cut the cheese into 12 slices. Knead the dough again on a lightly floured work surface and divide into 12 portions. Roll out each portion of dough into a round and place 1 tablespoon mushroom filling on each portion. Top with a slice of cheese.

Press the dough around the filling to enclose the filling completely, pressing the edges to seal. Brush about   of the melted butter over a rectangular baking sheet and place the rolls on the tray. Brush the rolls with the remaining butter, cover and set aside in a warm place until risen and doubled in size. Bake in a preheated oven at 400°F (200°C) for about 30 minutes. Serve warm or cold.

INGREDIENTS

FOR THE DOUGH

3 1/8 cups (395 g) strong plain wholemeal flour, 1 sachet dried yeast
1 tsp. sea salt, 2 eggs, 4 tbsp. soft butter
3/4 cup (6 fl. oz./175 ml) lukewarm yogurt

FOR THE FILLING

1 bunch of spring onions, 1 lb. 2 oz. (500 g) mushrooms, 2 tbsp. butter, sea salt
and freshly ground black pepper
1 tbsp. chopped fresh mixed herbs

3 1/2 oz. (100 g) mozzarella, mature Gouda or Cheddar cheese
3 tbsp. butter, melted

VARIATIONS

Use zucchinis or peppers in place of the mushrooms. Use Parmesan cheese for a change.

Onion and Caraway Seed Bread

Serves 8–12 people

62

PREPARATION

Place the rye, oats, and flour in a coffee mill together with 1 teaspoon caraway seeds and the coriander seeds and grind until fine. Place in a bowl. Carefully mix in the yeast and sourdough extract, then add the salt, soft butter, and 1 cup (8 fl. oz./237 ml) lukewarm water to the flour mixture. Mix well to form a dough, then knead for about 5 minutes, until smooth. Cover and set the dough aside in a warm place until risen and doubled in size.

Meanwhile, melt the unsalted butter in a pan and fry the onions until softened. Set aside to cool, then season with 1 teaspoon caraway seeds and the oregano. Knead the dough again on a lightly floured work surface and divide into 20 equal portions. Roll out each portion of dough until thin.

Grease a soufflé dish and cover the sides and bottom with 4 pieces of dough. Spoon a quarter of the onion mixture over the dough, then cover with 4 more pieces of dough. Continue in the same way until all the dough and onion mixture has been used up, finishing with a layer of dough. Press the layers together well, cover and set aside in a warm place for 30 minutes, until risen.

Brush the top of the dough with water and sprinkle with caraway seeds, then bake in a preheated oven at 400°F (200°C) for 1 hour. Remove the bread from the soufflé dish by tapping it and return the bread to the oven for a further 5 minutes. Serve warm or cold in slices.

INGREDIENTS

3/4 cup (156 g) rye
2/3 cup (100 g) oats
2 cups (250 g) strong plain white flour
2 tsp. caraway seeds, plus extra
for sprinkling
1 tsp. coriander seeds, 1 sachet dried yeast
1 packet sourdough extract
1 tsp. sea salt, 5 tbsp. soft butter
2 tbsp. unsalted butter
2 2/3 cups (300 g) onions, sliced
1 tsp. dried oregano

Calzone

INGREDIENTS

2 cups (300 g) strong plain white flour

1 sachet dried yeast

4 tbsp. olive oil

salt and freshly ground black pepper, 1/2 cup (4 fl. oz./118 ml) lukewarm milk

14 oz. (400 g) mushrooms

5 tomatoes, skinned

7 oz. (200 g) salami

4 slices (100 g) bacon

12 oz. (350 g) Gruyère cheese

1 onion, 8 tbsp. tomato purée

2 tbsp. fresh breadcrumbs

paprika, to taste, crushed garlic, to taste

garlic salt, to taste, chopped fresh oregano or marjoram, to taste

sunflower oil, for brushing, fresh herb sprigs, to garnish

PREPARATION

Sift the flour into a mixing bowl and stir in the yeast. Add the olive oil, 1 teaspoon salt, and milk, then knead to a smooth, workable dough. If the dough is too sticky, add a little more flour. Set aside the dough in a warm place until risen and doubled in size. Knead again and divide in half. Roll out each half of dough into a round and place on a greased baking sheet. Slice the mushrooms and tomatoes and set aside. Slice the salami, cut the bacon into pieces and cut the cheese into cubes. Slice the onion and set the ingredients aside. Mix the tomato purée and breadcrumbs together and add salt and pepper, paprika, and crushed garlic to taste. Spread the dough rounds with the tomato purée mixture, lay the sliced tomatoes on top and season with salt and pepper, paprika, and garlic salt to taste. Arrange the mushrooms, salami, bacon, cheese, and onion on top and sprinkle with pepper, paprika, and oregano or marjoram to taste. Fold the dough back over the filling and press edges to seal. Brush on sunflower oil and sprinkle on herbs. Bake in a preheated oven at 400°F (200°C) for 20–30 minutes, until cooked and golden brown. Serve hot, garnished with fresh herb sprigs.

Florentine Pizza Layer

Serves 6–8 people

PREPARATION

For the dough, mix the flour and yeast in a bowl with the olive oil, salt, lemon juice, and 1 cup (8 fl. oz./237 ml) lukewarm water and knead to a firm but workable dough. Brush with olive oil, cover, and set aside in a warm place for 1 hour, until risen. Divide the dough into 6 equal portions and roll out each one on a floured tea-towel to a round about 10 inches (25 cm) in diameter. Cover each round in cling film to prevent drying out.

For the filling, wash the spinach, then heat the sunflower oil in a frying pan and stir-fry the spinach until softened. Stir in the garlic and season to taste with salt and pepper. Thinly slice the tomatoes, chop the nuts and grate the cheese. Set aside.

Place one layer of dough in a greased flan tin with a loose-bottom, brush with about a quarter of the olive oil, and sprinkle with some Parmesan and chopped pine nuts. Lay some spinach on top of the dough and cover with some slices of tomato. Brush the second layer of dough with oil and lay the oiled side on the tomatoes. Bake on the middle shelf of a preheated oven at 475°F (240°C) for about 10 minutes.

Remove the first 2 layers from the oven and brush with olive oil and add a further layer of dough and filling as before, then bake for a further 10 minutes. Repeat this process to complete the remaining layers. Sprinkle the final layer with remaining cheese and whole pine nuts.

INGREDIENTS

FOR THE DOUGH

2 cups (300 g) strong plain wholemeal flour

1 sachet dried yeast

6 tbsp. olive oil, plus extra for brushing

1 tsp. salt, 1 tsp. lemon juice

FOR THE FILLING

4 lb. 8 oz. (2 kg) fresh spinach

1 tbsp. sunflower oil

1 clove garlic, thinly sliced

salt and freshly ground black pepper

1 lb. 2 oz. (500 g) tomatoes

5 tbsp. pine nuts

3 1/2 oz. (100 g) Parmesan cheese, plus 4 tbsp. finely grated

4 tbsp. olive oil

Egg and Salami Calzone

Serves 4–6 people

PREPARATION

Prepare the bread mix and dried yeast according to the instructions on the packet. Set the dough aside in a warm place for 15 minutes, until risen, then divide the dough in half and roll out each half to a round of about 8 ½ inches (21 cm) in diameter. Place one of the rounds on a greased baking sheet.

Remove the eggs from their shells. Cut the Gouda cheese into thin slices and cut the mini salamis into ½-inch (1 ¼ cm) slices. Sprinkle half the cheese over the dough round on the baking sheet, leaving a 1 ¼-inch (3 cm) border all round the edge.

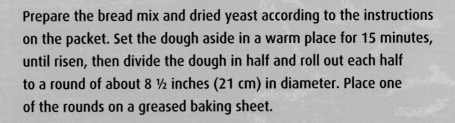

Place the eggs in the center, then arrange the salami between the eggs and the edge of the dough. Sprinkle over the remaining cheese and place the other dough round on top, pressing the edges down to seal. Brush the dough with water, cover, and set aside in a warm place for 30 minutes, until risen. Sprinkle the risen dough with flour and bake in a preheated oven at 400°F (200°C) for about 45 minutes, until cooked and golden brown. Serve hot.

INGREDIENTS

12 1/2 oz. (360 g) ready-to-use bread mix
1 sachet dried yeast
4 eggs, hard-boiled
7 oz. (200 g) Gouda cheese
6 mini salamis
plain flour, for sprinkling

SERVING SUGGESTION

Serve with fresh cooked vegetables such as green beans and baby corn cobs.

VARIATIONS

Use cooked smoked chicken or turkey in place of salami. Use Edam cheese in place of Gouda.

Olive Rolls

INGREDIENTS

FOR THE DOUGH

3 tbsp. fresh yeast
3 3/4 cups (600 g) strong plain wholemeal flour
3 tbsp. olive oil
3 tbsp. Italian dried mixed herbs
1 tsp. salt

FOR THE FILLING

5 1/2 oz. (150 g) stuffed green olives

5 1/2 oz. (150 g) shelled almonds
1 cup (200 g) ricotta cheese
1 cup (200 g) low-fat curd cheese
1 tbsp. Italian dried mixed herbs
1 red bell pepper, seeded and thinly sliced into strips

PREPARATION

For the dough, in a bowl dissolve the yeast in ½ cup (4 fl. oz./118 ml) lukewarm water and add the flour, a further 1 ¼ cup (10 fl. oz./300 ml) lukewarm water, the olive oil, dried herbs, and salt. Mix together and knead the ingredients to a pliable dough. Cover and set aside in a warm place for 1 hour, until risen and doubled in size.

For the filling, place the stuffed olives and almonds in a blender or food processor and blend until smooth. Mix the purée with the ricotta cheese, cottage cheese, and dried herbs. Set aside.

Divide the dough into 30 small round balls. Press your thumb into the dough balls to hollow out the centers and place them on a greased baking sheet. Spoon the almond paste into the hollow of each ball of dough and set aside in a warm place for about 15 minutes, until risen. Bake in the center of a preheated oven at 400°F (200°C) for about 25 minutes. Lay the pepper slices over the cooked olive rolls and serve hot.

Herb and Cheese Bread

Serves 6–8 people

PREPARATION

For the dough, mix the flours and yeast together in a bowl,
then add the salt, pepper and sugar. Add 1 cup (8 fl. oz./237 ml)
lukewarm water and mix well to form a dough.

Knead for about 5 minutes, until a smooth dough is formed.
Cover and set aside in a warm place until risen and doubled in size.
For the filling, melt the unsalted butter in a pan, add the onions,
and fry until softened. Remove the pan from the heat, stir in the egg,
grated cheese, and mixed herbs and mix well. Set aside. Sprinkle the risen
dough and work surface with flour and knead the dough again before
rolling it out to a rectangle about 12 x 16 inches (30 x 33 cm).

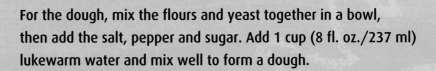

Spread the soft butter over the dough, then evenly spread the onion filling
over the dough leaving a border along the long edge free from filling.
From the short side of the rectangle, roll up the dough from both sides
towards the middle. Place the rolled-up dough in a greased bread
tin measuring about 12 x 4 ¼ inches (30 x 102 cm) and cut the top with
a knife in zigzags. Cover the dough and set aside in a warm place until
risen. Beat the egg yolk with 1 tablespoon water and brush the dough with
the mixture. Bake in a preheated oven at 375°F (190°C) for 40–50 minutes.

INGREDIENTS

FOR THE DOUGH

2 cups (255 g) strong plain
white flour
2 cups (255 g) strong plain
wholemeal flour
1 sachet dried yeast, 1 tsp. salt
freshly ground black pepper, to taste
1 tsp. sugar

FOR THE FILLING

1 tbsp. unsalted butter
2–3 onions, finely chopped
1 egg, 1 cup (100 g) Gouda
cheese, grated
5–6 tbsp. chopped fresh
mixed herbs, 1 tbsp. soft butter
1 egg yolk

Empanadas

INGREDIENTS

FOR THE DOUGH

2 2/3 cups (200 g) plain white or wholemeal flour
7/8 cup (200 g) cornflour
1/2 cup butter, 1 egg
1/4 tsp. salt

FOR THE FILLING

1 onion, 2 cloves garlic
2 beefsteak tomatoes, skinned
10 pitted black olives
3 1/2 oz. (100 g) mature Gouda cheese
2 tbsp. olive oil
9 oz. /255 g red beanshoots
2 tbsp. tomato purée, 6 pepperoni slices
2 tbsp. chopped parsley
salt and freshly ground black pepper
1 egg yolk, 1 tbsp. milk, fresh herb sprigs, to garnish

PREPARATION

For the dough, mix together the flour and cornflour in a bowl with the butter, egg, 1–2 tablespoons water, and salt to form a smooth, workable dough. Cover and set aside the dough to rest at room temperature for 1 hour. For the filling, peel the onion and garlic and thinly slice. Slice the tomatoes, chop the olives, and finely grate the cheese. Heat the oil in a pan and cook the onion, garlic, tomatoes, and olives for 5 minutes. Add the beanshoots and tomato purée and cook for about 10 minutes, stirring occasionally. Mash the mixture using a potato masher. Chop the pepperoni slices into small pieces and stir into the mashed mixture with the cheese, parsley and salt and pepper to taste. Roll out the dough to form rounds about ¼ inches (1 ¼ cm) thick and 4 ½ inches (11 cm) in diameter. Place some filling in the middle of each round. Fold the dough over itself and the filling to enclose, pressing the edges down to seal. Beat the egg yolk and milk together and brush the empanadas with the mixture. Place on a greased baking sheet and bake in a preheated oven at 400°F (200°C) for 15–20 minutes. Serve hot or cold, garnished with fresh herb sprigs.

Pumpkin Flan

Serves 4-6 people

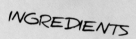

INGREDIENTS

FOR THE PASTRY

1 cup plus 1 tbsp. (255 g) plain flour
1 tsp. salt
1/2 cup (100 g) cold butter, diced

FOR THE FILLING

1 lb. 10 oz. (750 g) pumpkin flesh
1 cup (8 fl. oz./237 ml) dry cider

2 eggs, beaten
1 x 7-oz. (200 ml) carton creme fraiche
1/2 tsp. cayenne pepper
1 tsp. curry powder
juice of 1 lemon
10 1/2 oz. (300 g) boiled ham

PREPARATION

For the pastry, sift the flour and salt into a bowl and add the butter. Rub the butter into the flour using your fingertips until the mixture resembles breadcrumbs. Stir in enough cold water to form a smooth pastry. Cover and set aside to rest in the refrigerator for 30 minutes. Meanwhile, for the filling, cut the pumpkin flesh into cubes, place in a pan with the cider, bring to the boil, and simmer gently for 5 minutes, or until soft. Remove from the heat and drain immediately. Mash the pumpkin to a coarse purée, then stir in the eggs, creme fraiche, cayenne pepper, curry powder, and lemon juice. Dice the ham into cubes and stir into the pumpkin mixture, mixing well. Roll the pastry out thinly on a lightly floured work surface and use to line a 12-inch (25 cm) flan dish. Spoon in the pumpkin mixture and level the surface. Bake in the center of a preheated oven at 400°F (200°C) for about 50 minutes. Serve hot.

VARIATIONS

Use squash in place of pumpkin.
Use wine or stock in place of cider.

Lamb and Eggplant Flan

Serves 4 people

INGREDIENTS

2 lb. 4 oz. (1 kg) eggplant
3/4 cup (6 fl. oz./175 ml) olive oil
1 onion, 1 lb. 2 oz. (500 g) ground
lamb, 1 tbsp. chopped fresh thyme
1/4 cup (2 fl. oz./60 ml),
white wine, 7 oz. (200 g) tomatoes,
salt, 1/3 cup (70 g) Emmenthal
cheese, grated, 2 eggs,
1/2 cup (4 fl. oz./118 ml) heavy
cream, fresh herb sprigs,
to garnish

COOK'S TIP

Choose egg plants which are firm with
bright, shiny unwrinkled and unblemished
skins.

VARIATIONS

Use ground beef or pork in place of lamb.

PREPARATION

Wash the eggplants and cut into slices. Heat some of the olive oil in a frying pan and fry the eggplant slices a few at a time until lightly browned all over, adding more olive oil as required. Remove using a slotted spoon and set aside on a plate. Peel and finely chop the onion and add to the oil in which the eggplants have been cooked, then add the minced lamb and stir-fry until browned all over. Add the thyme and wine and stir to mix. Skin the tomatoes, remove and discard the seeds, cut them into chunks and add to the lamb. Season to taste with salt and mix well. Grease an ovenproof flan dish and cover the dish with a layer of eggplant slices. Mix the remaining eggplant slices with the lamb and spread the mixture over the first layer. Sprinkle the Emmenthal cheese over the lamb and eggplant mixture, then beat the eggs with the cream and pour over the top, covering the cheese completely. Cook, uncovered, for 15 minutes in a preheated hot oven at 400°F (200°C), then cover with foil and reduce the heat to 300°F (150°C) and cook for a further 45 minutes. Remove the foil towards the end of cooking to form a golden-brown crust. Serve hot, garnished with fresh herb sprigs.

Tomato Tart Isabelle

Serves 4-6 people

INGREDIENTS

FOR THE PASTRY

1 1/3 cups (170 g) plain white flour,
1/2 tsp. baking powder
salt, cold butter, diced

FOR THE FILLING

1 lb. 2 oz. (500 g) small tomatoes
salt and freshly ground black
pepper

7 oz. (200 g) Gruyère or
Emmenthal cheese
2 eggs
1 x 7-oz. (200 g) carton sour cream
ground nutmeg, to taste
1/2 tsp. dried oregano
fresh breadcrumbs, for sprinkling

PREPARATION

For the pastry, mix the flour and baking powder together and sift onto a work surface. Make a well in the middle and add salt, 1 tablespoon water and butter and cover with the flour. Working from the center, using you fingertips, mix to make a smooth pastry. If the pastry is sticky, chill for a while in the refrigerator.
Grease a 9 ½ inches (24 cm) loose-bottomed flan tin. Roll the pastry out on a lightly floured work surface and use to line the tin. Prick the base all over with a fork. Bake the flan case in a preheated oven at 400°F (200°C) for 12–15 minutes. Set aside. Meanwhile, for the filling, skin the tomatoes, slice the flesh in half, and lay on a plate with the cut sides upwards. Season to taste with salt and pepper and set aside for a few minutes, to allow the seasonings to be absorbed. Grate the cheese or cut into small cubes and mix with the eggs, sour cream, nutmeg, and oregano. Sprinkle the base of the flan case with breadcrumbs and arrange the tomatoes on top, cut-side down. Sprinkle the cheese mixture over the top and bake in the oven for 30–35 minutes. Serve hot or cold in slices.

Quiche Lorraine

Serves 4–6 people

INGREDIENTS

FOR THE PASTRY

2 cups (250 g) plain flour
1 egg yolk, pinch of salt
4 oz. (100g) cold butter

FOR THE FILLING

3 oz. (85 g) Gruyère cheese
6 slices bacon
1/2 cup (4 fl. oz./118 ml) half-and-half
4 eggs, salt and freshly ground black pepper,
grated nutmeg, to taste
fresh herb sprigs, to garnish

COOK'S TIP

Use a pair of clean kitchen scissors to snip the bacon quickly and easily into pieces.

PREPARATION

For the pastry, sift the flour onto a work surface. Make a well in the center, add the egg yolk, salt and 4 tablespoons water and knead to form a firm dough.

Cut the butter into cubes and add to the mixture, sprinkle with the flour and, working from the center using your fingertips, knead until a smooth pastry is formed. Grease a 9 ½ inch (24 cm) loose-bottomed flan tin. Roll the pastry out on a lightly floured work surface and use to line the tin. Prick the base of the flan case all over with a fork. Bake in a preheated oven at 400°F (200°C) for 15 minutes. Set aside.

For the filling, slice the cheese into thin strips and cut the bacon into small pieces. Fry the cheese and bacon together briefly in a pan, then remove the pan from the heat and stir in the cream, eggs and salt and pepper and nutmeg to taste, mixing well. Spoon the mixture into the flan case.

Bake in the oven for about 25 minutes, until golden brown. Serve warm or cold in slices, garnished with fresh herb sprigs.

Asparagus and Olive Quiche

Makes 2 quiches

INGREDIENTS

6 eggs
7/8 cups (7 fl. oz./207 ml)
half-and-half, 1 tsp. salt
pinch of grated nutmeg
salt and freshly ground black
pepper, 2 tbsp. plain flour
2 x 10 1/2-oz. (330 g) cans green
asparagus tips, drained,
6 oz. (175 g) green olives, 2 onions,
finely chopped and sautéed
in a little butter until soft

2 x 10-in. (25 cm)
part-baked pastry flan cases
6 tbsp. Cheddar cheese, grated, 2 tbsp.
Parmesan cheese, grated, 4 tbsp. butter

VARIATIONS

Use cooked green beans or mushrooms
in place of asparagus.

PREPARATION

In a bowl, whisk the eggs with the cream.
Add the salt, nutmeg, and seasoning.
Mix a little of the mixture with the flour until smooth,
then add to the cream mixture, mixing well.
Arrange the asparagus tips, olives, and onions
in the flan cases and pour the cream
mixture over the top. Sprinkle with
the grated Cheddar and Parmesan cheeses.
Dot with the butter and bake in a preheated
oven at 375°F (190°C) for 25 minutes.
Reduce the oven temperature to 350°F (180°C)
and bake for a further 15 minutes,
until the quiches are golden.
Serve warm or cold in slices.

Leek Flan

Serves 4–6 people

PREPARATION

Sift the flour onto a work surface and cut the butter into small cubes. Add the butter to the flour with the salt and sugar and knead the ingredients together to form a soft, workable pastry. Cover and place the pastry in the refrigerator to rest for 30 minutes. Roll out the pastry and use to line a loose-bottomed deep 11-inch (23 cm) flan tin. Prick the base all over with a fork. Bake in a preheated oven at 475°F (240°C) for 10 minutes. Set aside.

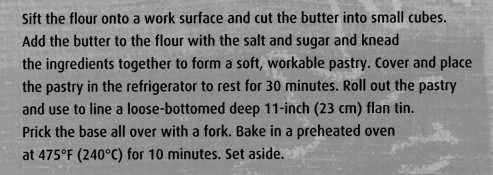

Reduce the oven temperature to 400°F (200°C). Meanwhile, cut the bacon into small pieces and fry in a pan until colored all over. Remove from the pan using a slotted spoon and place on a plate. Set aside.

Cook the leeks in the bacon fat for about 15 minutes, until softened, stirring occasionally. Remove from the heat, season with salt and pepper to taste, and set aside to cool. Mix the cottage cheese, herbs, and eggs with the cooked leeks and bacon and spoon the mixture into the flan case. Bake in the oven for 40 minutes. Serve hot in slices.

INGREDIENTS

2 cups (250 g) plain flour
1 cup (100 g) cold butter
1/2 tsp. salt
pinch of sugar
4 slices bacon
2 lb. 4 oz. (1 kg) leeks, washed and sliced
salt and freshly ground black pepper
7/8 cup (200 g) cottage cheese
1 tbsp. finely chopped fresh mixed herbs
3 eggs, lightly beaten

SERVING SUGGESTION

Serve with homemade coleslaw
and warm crusty bread.

Mini Leek and Bacon Flans

Makes 4 flans

INGREDIENTS

1 cup (125g) plain flour
1/4 tsp. salt, 5 tbsp. cold butter
3 1/2 oz. (100 g) Gruyère cheese,
cut into 4 slices
4 slices bacon, diced
2 leeks, washed and sliced
salt and freshly ground black
pepper
5 oz. (150 g) mozzarella cheese
fresh herb sprigs, to garnish

SERVING SUGGESTION
Serve with warm ciabatta rolls
and a mixed leaf salad.

VARIATIONS
Use blue cheese in place of Gruyère.
Use cooked chicken or turkey in place
of bacon.

PREPARATION

Sift the flour into a bowl, add the salt, cold butter and 2 tablespoon cold water and work the ingredients together to form a smooth pastry. Cover and place in the refrigerator for 30 minutes to rest. Sprinkle the pastry and work surface with flour, roll out the pastry and use to line 4 x4 inch (9 x 9 cm) flan tins.

Lay a slice of Gruyre cheese in the bottom of each flan case. Fry the bacon in a pan for 3 minutes, then add the leeks and cook for about 10 minutes, stirring occasionally. Season to taste with salt and pepper. Cut the mozzarella cheese into pieces. Divide the leek mixture and mozzarella equally between the flan cases. Bake in a preheated oven at 400°F (200°C) for 15–20 minutes. Serve hot or cold, garnished with fresh herb sprigs.

Mixed
Vegetable Flan

Serves 4–6 people

PREPARATION

Sift the flour into a bowl and make a well in the center. Add the salt,
1 egg, and the butter or margarine. Sprinkle the flour over the fat,
then blend all the ingredients together by hand to form a smooth pastry.
Cover and place in the refrigerator for 1–2 hours to rest.

Slice the zucchini and wash and slice the leek. Cook the zucchini, leek,
and mushrooms in a large saucepan of lightly salted, boiling water for
3 minutes. Drain well and set aside. Cook the broccoli in a pan of boiling
salted water for 3 minutes. Drain well and set aside. Slice the tomatoes
and set aside.

Roll out the pastry on a lightly floured work surface and use to line
a 10 ½–inch (26 cm) loose-bottomed flan tin. Prick the base all over
with a fork. Bake in a preheated oven at 400°F (200°C) for 10 minutes.
Place all the mixed vegetables in the flan case and season
with pepper and the dried herbs.

Chop the cheese into cubes and distribute evenly over the vegetables.
In a bowl, mix the creme fraiche with the mustard, the remaining
2 eggs, fresh herbs, and salt and nutmeg to taste. Adjust the seasoning,
then pour the sauce evenly over the filling. Bake in the oven
for 45 minutes. Serve hot or cold in slices.

INGREDIENTS

7/8 cup (200 g) plain wholemeal flour
1 tsp. salt, plus extra for seasoning
3 eggs, 1 cup (100 g) cold butter
or margarine, diced, 1 zucchini, 1 leek
7 oz. (200 g) mushrooms
10 1/2 oz. (300 g) frozen broccoli, 4 small
tomatoes, skinned, freshly ground black
pepper, to taste, dried Italian mixed herbs,
to taste, 7 oz. (200 g) Gouda cheese,
3/4 cup (6 fl. oz./77 ml) sour cream, 1 tsp.
mustard, 1 tbsp. chopped fresh mixed herbs,

grated nutmeg, to taste

SERVING SUGGESTION

Serve with crusty French bread
and a mixed salad.

VARIATIONS

Use cauliflower or asparagus
in place of broccoli.

Smoked Haddock and Egg Quiche

Serves 6 people

INGREDIENTS

8 oz. (225 g) wholemeal pastry
12 oz. (350 g) smoked haddock filet
3/4 cup (6 fl. oz./177 ml) chicken stock
2 hard-boiled eggs, chopped
1 tbsp. chopped fresh chives
6 tbsp. Cheddar cheese, grated
3 eggs, hard-boiled
1 1/2 cups (10 fl. oz./355 ml) milk
salt and freshly ground black pepper

VARIATION

Use flaked canned tuna in place of the smoked haddock.

PREPARATION

Roll out the pastry to fit a 9-inch-deep (23 cm) fluted flan dish. Press the edges up well and push the base down firmly. Prick the base all over with a fork and bake in a preheated oven at 375°F (190°C) for 15 minutes.

Pour the chicken stock into a saucepan, add the fish and poach gently for about 8 minutes, or until just tender. Drain the fish and flake the flesh into a bowl, discarding any skin and bones. Mix the chopped hard-boiled eggs, chives and cheese with the fish and spread the mixture evenly over the base of the flan case.

Beat together the eggs and milk and season to taste with salt and pepper. Pour over the fish mixture in the flan case. Bake in the oven for 25–30 minutes, or until the filling is set.

Tomato
Savory Flan

PREPARATION

Mix the flour and baking powder together on a work surface and add the butter in small pieces. Cover the butter with the flour, then add the curd cheese and work all the ingredients together to form a smooth pastry. Roll the pastry out to form a rectangle, fold in half, cover with foil and place in the refrigerator for 1 hour. Repeat this process 3 more times. Roll out the pastry on a lightly floured work surface and use to line a 11-inch (27 cm) flan tin.

Slice the tomatoes and dice the ham. Place the ham in the flan case. Lay the tomato slices over the top, overlapping, and season with salt and pepper. Sprinkle dried herbs over the top. Thinly slice the onion and crush the garlic.

In a bowl, add the onion and garlic to the creme fraiche with the eggs. Mix well. Season to taste with salt and pepper and pour the mixture evenly over the tomatoes. Bake in a preheated oven at 400°F (200°C) for about 1 hour. Serve hot or cold in slices, garnished with fresh herb sprigs.

INGREDIENTS

2 cups (255 g) plain flour
pinch of baking powder
2/3 cup (225 g) cold butter
2/3 cup (254 g) low-fat cottage cheese
2 lb. 4 oz. beefsteak tomatoes
7 oz. (200 g) boiled ham
salt and freshly ground black pepper
dried herbes de Provence, to taste
1 onion. 1 clove garlic, 1 cup (8 fl. oz./237 ml)
sour cream
2 eggs, lightly beaten
fresh herb sprigs, to garnish

SERVING SUGGESTION

Serve with warm focaccia or
ciabatta and a mixed green salad.

VARIATIONS

Use half white and half
wholemeal flour in place of all
white flour. Use cherry or plum
tomatoes in place of beefsteak
tomatoes.

Index